PRENTICE-HALL HISTORY OF MUSIC SERIES

H. WILEY HITCHCOCK, editor

MUSIC IN THE MEDIEVAL WORLD, *Albert Seay*
MUSIC IN THE RENAISSANCE, *Howard Mayer Brown*
BAROQUE MUSIC, *Claude V. Palisca*
MUSIC IN THE CLASSIC PERIOD, *Reinhard G. Pauly*
NINETEENTH-CENTURY ROMANTICISM IN MUSIC, *Rey M. Longyear*
TWENTIETH-CENTURY MUSIC: AN INTRODUCTION, *Eric Salzman*
FOLK AND TRADITIONAL MUSIC OF THE WESTERN CONTINENTS, *Bruno Nettl*
MUSIC CULTURES OF THE PACIFIC, THE NEAR EAST, AND ASIA, *William P. Malm*
MUSIC IN THE UNITED STATES: A HISTORICAL INTRODUCTION, *H. Wiley Hitchcock*